Bye-Bye, Binky

Julia Burgwinkel

PAGE PUBLISHING
Conneaut Lake, PA

First originally published by Page Publishing 2024

ISBN 979-8-89157-891-3 (pbk)
ISBN 979-8-89157-903-3 (digital)

Printed in the United States of America

To my sweet girls, Lily, Lyanna and
Luna, who inspire me every day.

When you are a baby,
you need me to sleep.

You suck me and hold me;
I'm there when you weep.

I soothe you and love you.
I watch as you grow;
but now that you're bigger,
you must let me go.

Because you think that you need me,
this might make you sad;

But you are big and strong,
and you still have your mom and dad.

As you get a little older
and become a little lady,

I get a little younger,
and become more like a baby.

Now I need my mommy,
and my daddy too.
When I don't get to see them,
it makes me feel so blue.

I want to be with my family,
and you with yours, be well.
But for me to be my happiest,
you must bid me a proper farewell.

I have to go bye-bye,
such a big girl you are.
Just know that I love you,
and I'm never too far!

About the Author

Julia Burgwinkel was raised in New Jersey and currently resides in Mississippi with her loving husband and children. She has always had a passion for literature and writes short stories in her spare time or when inspiration strikes.